Copyright © 2023 by Stenlake Publica

All rights reserved. No part of this book may be rep
in any manner without prior written permission from the copyright
owner except for the use of quotations in a book review.

ISBN: 9798375115047

Imprint: Independently published

Disclaimer: All answers are correct as of 16th November 2021.

Stenlake Publications presents:

Newcastle Crossword

Check out our other books:

Liverpool Crossword
Manchester United Crossword
Arsenal Crossword
Manchester City Crossword
Tottenham Hotspur Crossword
Chelsea Crossword
Leeds United Crossword
Leicester City Crossword
Rangers Crossword
Celtic Crossword
England Crossword

"I've turned down Barcelona, Inter Milan, Juventus and Manchester United to play here. I hope everyone already knows how much it means to me to play for Newcastle United."

- Alan Shearer

"I didn't come here for the culture or the climate, but I want to adapt. I have discovered Newcastle Brown Ale and my ambition is to speak Geordie as well as Peter Beardsley".

- David Ginola

"Kevin (Keegan) phoned and said, 'we're going back pal! We're going to change that club around'"

- Terry McDermott before him and Kevin Keegan took over in 1992

"For a figurehead and for the North East, Sir Bobby was huge, but for Newcastle United he was massive. There was just this aura about him, when he spoke to you, he knew what made you tick."

- Alan Shearer on Sir Bobby Robson

Contents Page

Round 1 - Founding & History	1
Round 2 - 1950/60s	3
Round 3 - 1970/80s	5
Round 4 - 1990s	7
Round 5 - 2000s	9
Round 6 - 2010s	11
Round 7 - 2020s	13
Round 8 - Stan Seymour & Joe Harvey	15
Round 9 - Managers	17
Round 10 - Jackie Milburn	19
Round 11 - Alan Shearer	21
Round 12 - St James' Park	23
Round 13 - Academy Graduates	25
Round 14 - Club Captains	27
Round 15 - Kevin Keegan	29
Round 16 - Peter Beardsley	31
Round 17 - Steve Harper & Shay Given	33
Round 18 - General I	35
Round 19 - General II	37
Round 20 - General III	39

Round 1 - Answers	42
Round 2 - Answers	43
Round 3 - Answers	44
Round 4 - Answers	45
Round 5 - Answers	46
Round 6 - Answers	47
Round 7 - Answers	48
Round 8 - Answers	49
Round 9 - Answers	50
Round 10 - Answers	51
Round 11 - Answers	52
Round 12 - Answers	53
Round 13 - Answers	54
Round 14 - Answers	55
Round 15 - Answers	56
Round 16 - Answers	57
Round 17 - Answers	58
Round 18 - Answers	59
Round 19 - Answers	60
Round 20 - Answers	61

Round 1 - Founding & History

Newcastle United were founded in 1892 after the merger of two local clubs and were elected to the Football League a year later. The club dominated English football for 10 years in the early 20th century winning three league titles and an FA Cup in that time. They went on to add another league title and five FA Cups pre-WWII. This crossword covers the first 58 years of the club's history.

Across

2. Newcastle lost the 1905 FA Cup Final against this Midlands team, preventing them from doing the double. (5,5)

7. Newcastle defeated this London club to lift their third FA Cup in 1932.

8. The replay of the 1910 FA Cup final was held in this stadium. (8,4)

9. Newcastle were beaten by this team nicknamed 'The Toffees' in the 1906 FA Cup.

12. The first man to score 100 goals for the club. (4,6)

13. Hughie Gallacher left Newcastle for this London club in 1930.

15. First official manager of Newcastle who was appointed in 1930. (4,10)

16. Newcastle lost their maiden First Division game against this Midlands side. (13,9)

17. This player made a club-record 496 appearances from 1904-1921. (5,8)

18. Defender that made 330 appearances for the club who Jackie Milburn described as "the best uncapped fullback I've ever known". (5,6)

19. Newcastle lost against this club nicknamed 'The Bantams' in the 1911 FA Cup Final. (8,4)

20. Neil Harris and this future manager were the goal scorers in the 1924 FA Cup Final. (4,7)

Down

1. Newcastle won their first FA Cup in 1910 by defeating this Yorkshire club in the final.

3. At the beginning of the 1893/94 season Newcastle were refused entry into the First Division with Woolwich Arsenal and this Merseyside club.

4. From 1892 to 1929, the team was selected by a committee represented by this man. (5,4)

5. Newcastle was formed after Newcastle East End merged with this club in 1892. (9,4,3)

6. Club captain for the 1926/27 title-winning season. (6,9)

10. Newcastle's first competitive game was against this club, who are still a modern-day local rival.

11. Newcastle's record win of 13-0 came against this Welsh club in 1946. (7,6)

14. Former left-half who famously quoted "The Newcastle team of the 1900s would give any modern side a two goal start and beat them, and furthermore, beat them at a trot." (5,9)

Round 2 - 1950/60s

The club had a successful spell at the start and end of this period either side of a spell in the Second Division. The Magpies won three FA Cups in 5 years between 1951 and 1955. They also won their first and only European trophy in 1969 via the old Inter-Cities Fairs Cup which is regarded as the frontrunner to the UEFA Cup.

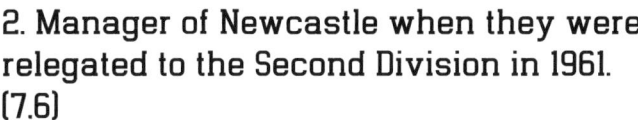

Across

1. Northern Irish goalkeeper for the 1969 Inter-Cities Fairs Cup who made over 300 appearances for the club in total. (6,6)

7. Chilean who scored the winning goal in the 1952 FA Cup Final. (6,7)

9. Side defeated in the 1952 FA Cup Final.

13. Scotsman and cult hero who made most of his 129 appearances in the 1960s and later became a postman in the Lake District. (4,8)

14. Prime minister who handed Joe Harvey the 1952 FA Cup to lift. (7,9)

15. Wyn Davies was signed by Newcastle in 1966 from this club, nicknamed 'The Trotters'. (6,9)

16. Legendary striker who scored both goals in the final of the 1951 FA Cup. (6,7)

17. Newcastle beat Újpest of this country to win the 1969 Inter-Cities Fairs Cup.

18. Manager who was in charge of Newcastle when they qualified for their first European competition. (3,6)

19. Dutch side who Newcastle beat in the first round of the 1968/69 Inter-Cities Fairs Cup.

Down

2. Manager of Newcastle when they were relegated to the Second Division in 1961. (7,6)

3. Newcastle's third highest goal scorer of all time with 153 goals in 269 appearances. (3,5)

4. Scored the most goals for Newcastle during the 1955 FA Cup campaign and wore Jackie Milburn's number 9 shirt in the final (Milburn wore 8). (3,6)

5. Played 464 games for the club before winning the European Cup with Nottingham Forest. (5,5)

6. Scottish side who Newcastle beat in the semi-finals of the 1968/69 Inter-Cities Fairs Cup.

8. Newcastle defeated this Lancashire team in the 1952 FA Cup semi-final after a replay. (9,6)

10. Scored a brace in the first leg of the 1969 Inter-Cities Fairs Cup Final against Újpest. (5,6)

11. Welsh Sports Hall of Fame inductee who moved to Newcastle from Swansea Town in 1958.

12. Side defeated in the 1955 FA Cup Final. (10,4)

15. Newcastle won the 1951 FA Cup Final by defeating this team led by Stanley Matthews.

Round 3 - 1970/80s

The 70s and 80s were a difficult period for the club as they bounced between the First and Second Division. There were a few high points however, including an FA Cup Final in 1974, two Texaco Cups and an Anglo-Italian Cup.

Across

1. Paul Gascoigne left Newcastle to join this club in 1988. (9,7)

4. Malcolm Macdonald scored a hat-trick against this club on his home debut in 1971.

7. Stan Seymour once described this player as "George Best without brains". (4,9)

8. Newcastle lifted the 1975 Texaco Cup by defeating this South Coast team in the final.

14. Kevin Keegan made his Newcastle debut against this London club in 1982. (6,4,7)

17. This former Newcastle manager appeared in the 1981 film Escape to Victory. (5,7)

18. Local lad signed as a 19-year-old in July 1980 for £1,000 who went on to win 62 caps for England. (5,6)

19. Newcastle lifted the 1974 Texaco Cup by defeating this Lancashire team in the final who they also beat in the FA Cup semi-final that year.

Down

2. Striker who was bought for a record £180,000 in 1971 and was nicknamed "Supermac". (7,9)

3. Nickname of Francisco Ernandi Lima Da Silva who represented Newcastle from 1987-1989.

5. Northumberland-born World Cup winner who took over as manager in 1984. (4,8)

6. Liverpudlian striker who made the Second Division team of the year in both his seasons at the club in 1979 and 1980. (5,5)

8. Future manager who scored against Newcastle in an FA Cup fifth round tie in 1975/76 season for Bolton Wanderers. (3,9)

9. Scored a hat-trick in the Tyne-Wear derby on New Year's Day 1985. (5,9)

10. Irish midfielder who won the club's player of the year award in 1982. (4,6)

11. Newcastle were defeated by this team in the 1974 FA Cup Final.

12. Scored Newcastle's only goal as they lost 2-1 against Manchester City in the 1976 League Cup Final. (4,7)

13. Kevin Keegan's strike partner in the 1982/83 season before Peter Beardsley replaced him. (4,6)

15. Malcolm MacDonald set a club record of the fastest goal from kickoff against this Scottish club in 1972. (2,9)

16. This player set a club record of the quickest sending off in Newcastle's history in a Texaco Cup match against Birmingham City in 1974. (5,5)

Round 4 - 1990s

The 90s were the club's most successful period in recent history having gone from the Second Division to Premier League runners-up in just four seasons. They would get agonisingly close to their first Premier League title again in the following season before reaching back-to-back FA Cup Finals. Some of the club's greatest players graced the St James' Park pitch during this decade.

Across

1. Part of the famous Class of '92 to emerge at Manchester United who joined Newcastle in 1995. (5,9)

4. Georgian signed from AEK Athens in 1997. (5,8)

5. Faustino Asprilla was signed from this Italian club in 1996.

6. Club that Stuart Pearce spent 12 seasons at before joining Newcastle. (10,6)

9. Scored a stunning chip in a 5-0 demolition of Manchester United in 1996. (8,6)

12. Club that Newcastle beat 8-0 in the league in 1999. (9,9)

14. Holds the club record of scoring the most goals in a single campaign notching 41 in the 1993/94 season. (4,4)

16. Robert Lee was signed in 1992 from this London club. (8,8)

17. Alan Shearer hit a 13-minute hat-trick including a last-minute winner as Newcastle came from 3-1 down against this club in February 1997. (9,4)

18. Newcastle famously beat this Spanish opposition in the Champions League in September 1997.

19. Striker signed from Derby in 1994 for £2.25m. (4,6)

20. Croatian international signed from Croatia Zagreb in 1998 but lasted one season before joining Porto. (6,5)

Down

2. Player who had two spells for Newcastle and played for Manchester United, Manchester City, Liverpool and Everton. (5,9)

3. Newcastle lost the 1999 FA Cup final against this club. (10,6)

7. Steve Howey left Newcastle for this club in 1999. (10,4)

8. Shirt sponsors from 1995 to 2000. (9,5,3)

10. The youngest debutant in the club's history. (5,5)

11. Midfielder signed from arch rivals Sunderland in 1992. (4,9)

13. He wore Newcastle's number nine shirt for the 1995/96 season. (3,9)

15. This player was signed from PSG in 1998 and sold back there three years later. (6,4)

Round 5 - 2000s

The 2000s were a mixed bag for the club with some fantastic European nights, a few top 5 finishes and an Intertoto Cup win in 2006. However, one of the darkest moments in the club's history came in 2009 when the club were relegated from the Premier League for the first time.

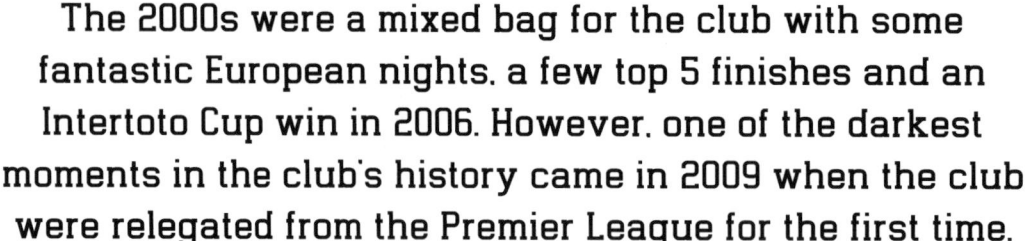

Across

3. Shola Ameobi scored his first ever hat-trick against this club in 2009.

4. Striker. famous for his somersault celebrations who signed in 2000. (6.6)

5. Peruvian who calls himself an 'adopted Geordie' after nine seasons at the club. (8.6)

7. Won the PFA Young Player of the Year in 2002 while playing for Newcastle. (5.7)

11. Player who scored a sublime dipping volley against Spurs in December 2003. (7.6)

15. Voted as Newcastle's Player of the Year for the 2008/2009 season. (9.7)

17. Member of the 'Class of '92' who signed in 2004. (5.4)

18. Alan Shearer scored *That* volley against this opposition in December 2002.

19. Kit manufacturer for the whole 2000s.

20. Succeeded Alan Shearer as captain in 2006. (5.6)

Down

1. Kieron Dyer was involved in an on-pitch brawl with this teammate in a match against Aston Villa in April 2005. (3.6)

2. Scored the only goal of the 2004/05 FA Cup fifth and sixth rounds against Chelsea and Spurs respectively. (7.8)

6. Took over Alan Shearer's number nine jersey after he retired. (7.7)

8. Won the PFA Young Player of the Year of 2003 while playing for Newcastle. (7.5)

9. Aussie who was manager Sam Allardyce's first signing for Newcastle in 2007. (4.6)

10. Signed from Manchester United for £6m in 2007. (4.5)

12. Graeme Souness broke the club's transfer record to sign this player at the start of the 2004/05 season for £16.8m. (7.4)

13. Newcastle bought Michael Chopra from this club in 2006. (7.4)

14. Striker who in 2007. was tipped by Gianluigi Buffon to have a big future after he scored against Juventus in 2007. (4.6)

16. Shirt sponsor from 2003-2012. (8.4)

Round 6 - 2010s

This decade started with an immediate return to the Premier League before achieving an excellent 5th place finish just two seasons later. Unfortunately, it was all downhill from there culminating in another relegation in 2016. However, Rafa and his men again won the Championship title at the first time of asking and the club have managed to stabilise since.

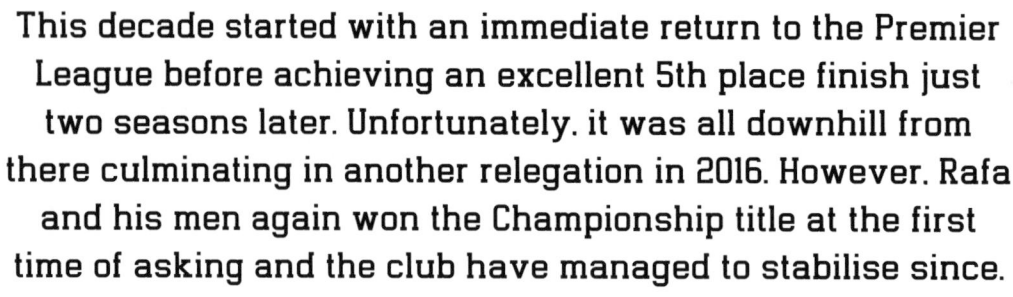

Across

3. Newcastle player who set a Premier League record of being the first player to receive five yellow cards in the first five league games in 2010/2011. (5,5)

4. Newcastle paid £40m for this player in 2019.

6. Scored Newcastle's first goal as they came from 4-0 down to draw with Arsenal. (4,6)

8. Voted as Newcastle's Player of the Year for 2018/2019. (7,6)

9. The youngest player to represent Newcastle in European competition at 17 years 236 days against Atromitos in 2012. (4,8)

11. The only Newcastle player to be voted in the PFA Team of the Year during the 2010s. (8,9)

12. Captained Newcastle to the Championship title in 2010. (5,5)

14. He became only the second player after Ryan Giggs to play in the first 19 seasons of the Premier League when he played for Newcastle against Manchester City in 2010. (3,8)

15. Club that Georginio Wijnaldum scored four goals against in a Premier League game. (7,4)

17. Newcastle's top scorer in the 2010s. (5,5)

18. Top scorer in the 2013/14 season. (4,4)

19. Newcastle player who represented the Netherlands at the 2014 World Cup. (3,4)

Down

1. Scored Newcastle's equaliser in their miraculous 4-4 comeback with Arsenal. (5,5)

2. Scored a hat-trick on his first Premier League start as Newcastle demolished West Ham 5-0 in January 2011. (4,4)

5. Jonas Gutierrez scored in his final game for the club against this team.

6. Voted as Newcastle's Player of the Year for 2017/2018. (6,8)

7. The most prolific goals per game scorer in a season for Newcastle is 13 goals in 14 matches during the 2011/12 season from this player. (6,5)

10. Top scorer in the 2016/17 title-winning season. (6,5)

13. Newcastle received their highest transfer fee after selling this player in 2011. (4,6)

16. Newcastle had 3 players representing this nation at the 2014 World Cup.

Round 7 - 2020s

The 2020s are promising to be one of the most exciting in the club's history. After a 12th and 13th place finish, the Mike Ashley era was over after the long-awaited Saudi-backed takeover of the club was completed in 2021. Overnight, the Magpies became the richest club on the planet, and it is only a matter of time before major honours return to St James'.

Across

2. Ryan Fraser was signed from this club in 2020 on a free transfer.

6. Club captain since 2016. (5,9)

9. County that former manager Steve Bruce was born in.

10. National team of Miguel Almiron.

11. Kit manufacturer for the 2021/22 season.

12. Chairman appointed in 2021. (5,2,8)

13. Player sold to Al-Raed in July 2021. (9,4)

14. Sleeve sponsor for the 2021/22 season.

17. Allan Saint-Maximin scored a late solo winner against this League 1 team in the FA Cup in 2020. (6,6)

18. This team knocked Newcastle out of the League Cup at the quarter-final stage in the 2020/2021 season.

19. National team of Martin Dubravka.

20. Steve Bruce's assistant manager. (5,5)

Down

1. Signed on loan from Arsenal in January 2021 and he went on to score 8 goals in 14 appearances. (3,7)

3. This player scored the only goal as Newcastle beat Manchester United at St. James' Park in the 2019/20 season. (5,9)

4. Voted the club's Player of the Year for the 2020/2021 season. (6,6)

5. Newcastle signed this player from Norwich City in September 2020. (5,5)

7. Business woman who led the Saudi takeover of Newcastle and owns a 10% stake. (6,8)

8. Team defeated on the opening game of the 2020/2021 season. (4,3,6)

15. Newcastle were knocked out of the FA Cup in the 2020/2021 season by this club.

16. Appointed manager in 2021. (5,4)

Round 8 - Stan Seymour & Joe Harvey

Two of Newcastle's all-time great players and managers are Stan Seymour and Joe Harvey. They racked up over 1400 games between them over their Newcastle careers with Seymour winning a First Division title and an FA Cup as a player before managing a Harvey-led side to two more FA Cups in the 50s. They have undoubtedly earned legendary status among the toon army.

Across

3. Yorkshire club that Harvey and Seymour both played for. (8.4)

4. Harvey initially applied for the managerial job at Newcastle in 1958 but lost out to this man. (7.6)

8. Harvey signed this player from Sheffield United who turned out to be an outstanding strike partner for Malcolm Macdonald. (4.5)

13. Harvey began his career at this Midlands club. (13.9)

15. Name of Seymour's son who became chairman and later director of Newcastle.

16. Harvey's final game for Newcastle was against this Midlands club. (5.5)

18. Manager that Seymour appointed in 1954 after he became vice-chairman. (4.11)

19. Seymour's playing position. (4.6)

20. Harvey won this cup as manager of Newcastle in the 1968/69 season. (5.3)

Down

1. Seymour gave a trial to this 19-year-old who went on to become a club legend himself. (6.7)

2. Seymour spent eight years as a player at this Scottish club, nicknamed 'The Ton', before joining Newcastle in 1920. (8.6)

5. Young full-back that Harvey gave a first team debut to who went on to win five First Division titles and two European Cups with Liverpool. (4.7)

6. This former Newcastle manager and player wanted to rename the club's youth academy after Seymour. (5.6)

7. After retiring as a player, Harvey took coaching courses from this man (England's first ever manager) (6.12)

9. Harvey has been described as a manager who had a flaw tactically but had man-management skills on a par with this legendary Scottish manager. (4.8)

10. Seymour was born in the village of Kelloe which is in this county. (6.6)

11. After a disagreement with Newcastle's officials, Seymour turned down the chance to continue his playing career by joining this local rival.

12. Harvey paid Sheffield Wednesday a club record £200,000 to sign this player in 1974.

14. Harvey's playing position. (4.4)

17. Seymour's name 'Stan' comes from his middle name, Stanley. This is his real first name.

Round 9 - Managers

The club have had a whole host of other managers throughout their history with varying degrees of success. Here are 20 clues about some of these men.

Across

2. Former manager who is the only in history to have won the UEFA Cup, UEFA Super Cup, UEFA Champions League and FIFA Club World Cup. (4,7)

3. Former player who replaced Charlie Mitten as coach in 1962. (3,6)

5. The first Irishman appointed as permanent manager of Newcastle. (3,7)

6. Popular local assistant coach who took over on an interim basis in 2015. (4,6)

7. Won both the Premier League Manager of the Season and the LMA Manager of the Year awards for the 2011-12 season (4,6)

9. Replaced Kevin Keegan as Newcastle manager after he resigned in 1998. (5,7)

14. Taken charge of the most Newcastle matches in the Premier League era. (5,6)

20. Newcastle's fifth manager. (4,11)

Down

1. Handed Paul Gascoigne his first team debut in 1985. (4,8)

4. Manager from 1975-77. (7,6)

8. This former player briefly left his role as a pundit for the BBC to become Newcastle's manager for the last eight games of the 2008/09 season. (4,7)

10. Manager who signed Michael Owen. (6,7)

11. Manager sacked in 2010 to the anger of the players and supporters. (5,7)

12. The first man to manage Sunderland and Newcastle. (3,9)

13. Led Newcastle to the 2006 Intertoto Cup title. (5,6)

15. Kevin Keegan took over as manager from this Argentine. (5,7)

16. Led Newcastle to the 1976 League Cup Final. (6,3)

17. Manager who led Scotland to Euro 2020 that was caretaker for one game in 1999. (5,6)

18. Dutchman who managed the club in the 90s. (4,6)

19. Replaced Andy Cunningham as manager of Newcastle in 1934 making him the second manager in Newcastle's history. (3,6)

Round 10 - Jackie Milburn

Jackie Milburn is arguably Newcastle's greatest player of the 20th century having scored 201 goals in 399 appearances for the club over 12 seasons. He was the first footballer to be made a Freeman of the City of Newcastle upon Tyne and was voted the 'greatest post-war North East footballer' by the local press in 1987. He was part of the side that won three FA Cups in the 50s.

Across

2. Milburn made guest appearances for this Yorkshire club during the war. (9.6)

4. He is the cousin of the mother of these brothers who won the World Cup with England.

5. Milburn was a sports journalist for this now-defunct newspaper. (4.2.3.5)

8. Milburn was a boyhood fan of this club who he made two guest appearances for in the 1945/45 season.

10. Milburn scored his 100th competitive goal for Newcastle against this Lancashire club.

11. Manager who gave Milburn all thirteen of his England caps.

18. After Milburn retired he briefly managed this Suffolk club. (7.4)

19. In the 1945/46 season Milburn was shifted from right-wing to accommodate this new signing. (7.6)

20. England and Preston legend who Milburn played alongside in all but one of his England caps. (3.6)

Down

1. Stan Seymour said of signing Milburn "I had secured my finest ever signing for ten quid and a couple of rounds of_____" this alcohol. (9.5.3)

3. Milburn scored the fastest FA Cup final goal, at the time, at Wembley in 1955 against this team. (10.4)

6. This Chelsea player, in 1997, broke Milburn's record of scoring the fastest ever FA Cup Final goal at Wembley. (7.2.6)

7. Manager who made the decision to switch Milburn to a centre forward. (6.6)

9. This Hungarian great featured In Milburn's testimonial. (6.6)

12. Legendary Newcastle player and manager who scored a brace for Bradford City against Newcastle on Milburn's debut. (3.6)

13. The man overtook Milburn as Newcastle's all-time leading goalscorer. (4.7)

14. He was also known as this (particularly in North East England, a Geordie dialectal). (3.6)

15. Milburn was born in this Northumberland town, famous for producing many great players.

16. Milburn was player-manager for this Northern Irish club after leaving Newcastle.

17. He idolized this legendary Arsenal winger while growing up. (3.5)

Round 11 - Alan Shearer

The greatest goal scorer in the history of Newcastle United and the Premier League is none other than local lad Alan Shearer. He scored 206 goals in 405 appearances over 10 seasons for the club and scored a total of 260 goals in the Premier League, a record that's still standing 15+ years after retiring. He was the first inductee into the Premier League Hall of Fame and was given Honorary Freedom of the City of Newcastle upon Tyne.

Across

3. He won the Premier League with this club before joining Newcastle. (9,6)

5. He scored his first Newcastle hat-trick against this club in 1997. (9,4)

7. He scored the winner against this side in the 1998 FA Cup semi-final. (9,6)

8. He replaced this player as captain of Newcastle in the 1998/99 season. (3,3)

9. He shares the record of scoring 5 goals in a Premier League game with this former Magpie among others. (4,4)

12. He scored 5 Premier League goals in one game against this club in 1999. (9,9)

13. He scored his final competitive goal against this club.

15. Manager who gave Shearer his England debut. (6,6)

17. His testimonial for Newcastle was against this club.

18. He was signed for this many million pounds.

19. He scored his only hat-trick for England against this country in September 1999.

Down

1. Famous youth club that Shearer played for which has produced over 65 professionals and multiple England internationals. (8,4,4)

2. In 1988, he became the youngest hat-trick scorer in English top-flight history at the age of 17 years 240 days, beating the record held for 30 years by this Spurs and England legend. (5,7)

4. An incident between this Irishman and Shearer led to the Manchester United player receiving a red card at St James' in the 2001/02 season. (3,5)

6. Bobby Robson tried to sign Shearer for this club for £20m in 1997.

7. He is a product of this club's academy.

10. He scored two hat-tricks for Newcastle in the Champions League, one against Hapoel Sakhnin and this German club. (5,10)

11. Scotsman who managed Shearer at two different clubs during his career. (5,8)

14. He scored his record-breaking 201st Newcastle goal against this club in 2006.

16. In a recent interview with Gary Neville, Shearer said that this away ground had the best atmosphere and was his favourite to play at.

Round 12 - St James' Park

St James's Park has been the home of Newcastle United for their entire history. After many developments through the decades, it now stands at a capacity of 52,305 making it the eighth largest football stadium in England. It has also hosted England internationals, Olympic matches, Rugby World Cup games and the Rugby League magic weekend among others.

Across

3. Businessman who used his experience in property development to gain approval and invest heavily in St James' Park. (4.4)

5. St James' Park missed out on hosting World Cup matches in 1966 due to planning difficulties and instead World Cup fixtures went to this North East stadium. (8.4)

6. Opponents in England's last international played at St James' Park in 2005.

8. Stand previously known as the Newcastle Brown Ale Stand. (10.3)

10. Name of the famous Scottish architect who designed St James' Park as well as many other famous grounds around the UK. (9.6)

13. Temporary name of the stadium from November 2011 to encourage sponsorship. (6.6.5)

15. The first floodlit game at St James' Park was against this Scottish team.

16. He was the first Royal to watch a match at St James' Park in 1932. (4.6.4)

17. The first competitive game at the newly redeveloped St James' Park in August 2000 was against this Midlands team. (5.6)

18. Eventual winners of the 2012 Olympics who played a group game against South Korea at St James'.

19. St James' hosted this nation twice at the 2015 Rugby Union World Cup.

20. A statue of this former manager is located on the south west corner of the ground. (5.6)

Down

1. Name for the open terracing that stood on the site of the present East Stand. (3.7.4)

2. This band were the first major rock band to play at St James' Park. (3.7.6)

4. Name of the stand where the away fans are seated. (6.3)

7. His statue was erected outside St James' Park in 2016. (4.7)

9. The West Stand is named after this former player. (6.7)

11. The last match before the old Leazes End 'singing end' was used before demolition was against this club. (10.4)

12. St James' Park hosted the 2002 World Cup Qualifying match between England and this nation.

14. Name of the road in front of the main entrance. (7.4)

Round 13 - Academy Graduates

The Newcastle academy is renowned for producing great talents. Can you name this select group of 20 players based on these clues?

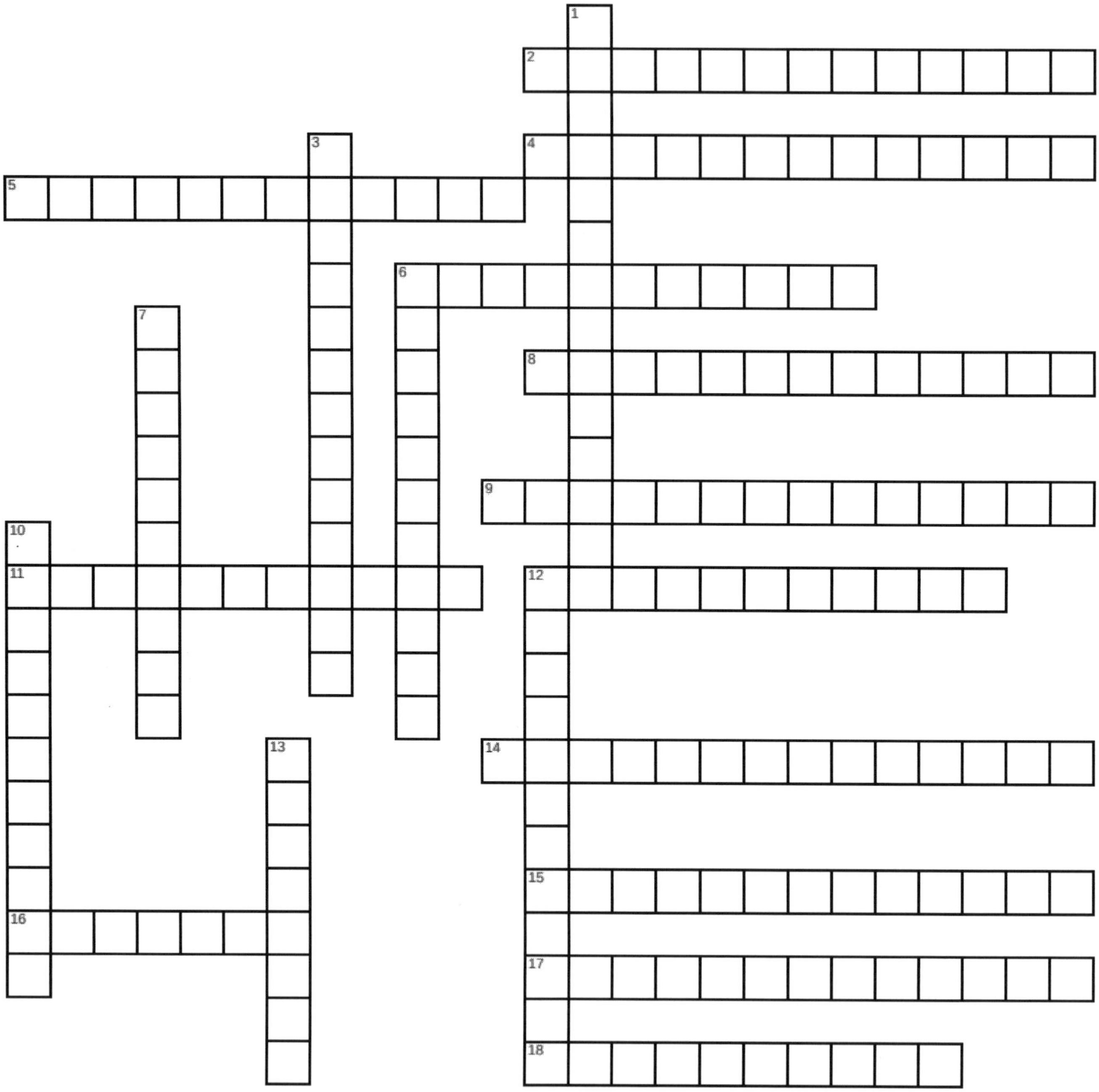

Across

2. Future England international goalkeeper who left in 2012 without making an appearance. (6,7)

4. Signed for Southampton from Blackburn in 2021 for £15 million. (4,9)

5. Remembered for a bizarre incident in 2005 where he "saved" Darius Vassell's shot and went down clutching his chest before being dismissed for "deliberate handball". (6,6)

6. The youngest player to play for the Newcastle first team having made his debut against Wolves in 1990.

8. Had two spells at Newcastle in between four seasons at Bolton before a spell at Sunderland. (6,7)

9. Captained Rangers to their 55th league title in the 2020/21 season. (5,8)

11. Northern Irishman who was never sent off in any of his 455 Premier League appearances. (5,6)

12. Scored for England against Sweden at Euro 2012. (4,7)

14. Scottish centre-back who spent six seasons at Newcastle before joining Sunderland and is now assistant coach of the Canadian national team. (6,8)

15. Striker of half Indian descent best known for his time at Cardiff City. (7,6)

16. Dutchman who made over 180 appearances for the club (3,4)

17. Midfielder who scored in the 1-1 draw with Watford in September 2021. (4,9)

18. Striker who had many run-ins with the law throughout his career including spending time in prison for fraud in 2017. (4,6)

Down

1. Goalkeeper who made 95 appearances in two seasons on loan at Swansea and is the godson of Gareth Southgate. (7,7)

3. Scored a memorable goal against Scotland at Euro '96. (4,9)

6. Nigerian international striker who represented Newcastle for 14 years. (5,6)

7. Popular figure who was a part of England's Euro '96 squad but failed to make an appearance. (5,5)

10. Newcastle-born Wales international who has spent his whole career at the club bar two loan spells. (4,7)

12. Midfielder best known for his time at Bolton and Celtic and won a sole England cap in 2004. (4,8)

13. Then-Sunderland player spotted with the Newcastle fans at the 1999 FA Cup wearing a T-shirt with the slogan "Sad Mackem Bastards". He never played for Sunderland again. (3,4)

Round 14 - Club Captains

The club have had many legendary captains in their history. Can you name the last 20 based on their years as captain as well as the number of appearances and goals for the club?

27

Across

7. 1982-84 - 85 apps. 49 goals. (5,6)

11. 1998-2006 - 405 apps. 206 goals. (4,7)

12. 2011-16 - 275 apps. 7 goals. (8,9)

14. 1994-97 - 326 apps. 119 goals. (5,9)

16. 1989-91 - 65 apps. 1 goal. (3,6)

17. 1978-79 - 228 apps. 12 goals. (5,7)

19. 1975-78 - 127 apps. 14 goals. (5,5)

20. 1991-92 - 274 apps. 11 goals. (5,5)

Down

1. 1979-82 - 147 apps. 5 goals. (4,6)

2. 2. 2007-08 - 54 apps. 3 goals.

3. 2008-09 - 79 apps. 30 goals. (7,4)

4. 2006-07 - 73 apps. 6 goals. (5,6)

5. 1984-88 - 219 apps. 8 goals. (5,6)

6. 1993-94 - 133 apps. 1 goal. (5,7)

8. 1992-93 - 45 apps. 0 goals. (5,8)

9. 1988-89 - 43 apps. 3 goals. (4,5)

10. 2016-present - 187 apps. 12 goals and counting. (6,9)

13. 2009-10 - 173 apps. 5 goals. (5,4)

15. 2010-11 - 91 apps. 30 goals. (5,5)

18. 1997-98 - 381 apps. 56 goals. (3,3)

Round 15 - Kevin Keegan

Kevin Keegan made quite the impression amongst the toon army despite just two years as a player and five as manager in his first spell. His passion and charisma were evident through his career making him a very popular figure amongst fans. He managed the club through a great period in the 90s and was agonisingly close to bringing the Premier League title to St James'

Across

4. Club that Newcastle signed him from.

5. Manager who signed him for Newcastle. (6.3)

6. He briefly came out of retirement to play a two-game stint for Blacktown City who are based in this country.

8. Liverpool replaced Keegan with this player who also replaced him as manager of Newcastle in 1997. (5.6)

11. Complete the quote "By the time I started playing for Newcastle, I had played against Cruyff, Maradona and Pelé, and yet I have never had my mind blown as I did on the first day I saw _____ _____." (5.9)

12. He began his career at this club, nicknamed 'The Iron'. (10.6)

15. 13-year-old future Newcastle captain who was a ballboy at Keegan's testimonial. (4.7)

16. Welshman who was Keegan's strike partner at Liverpool. (4.7)

17. Nickname given to him by Newcastle fans. (4.3)

18. He supported this Yorkshire club as a boy. (9.6)

19. Team he took charge of between 2001 and 2004. (10.4)

20. His ancestors arrived in England from this country.

Down

1. Legendary manager who signed Keegan for Liverpool. (4.7)

2. Keegan was given the England captaincy by this manager. (3.5)

3. He popularised this haircut style in the 80s.

7. Keegan scored twice against this team in the 1974 FA Cup Final. (9.6)

9. Club who Keegan lost to in the 1980 European Cup Final. (10.6)

10. He was the first Englishman to win the Ballon d'Or since this man. (5.8)

13. Frenchman that Keegan signed in 1995. (5.6)

14. Keegan joined this club after leaving Liverpool.

Round 16 - Peter Beardsley

Local lad who is one of the most talented players to grace the Newcastle shirt. He scored 119 goals in 326 games across two spells for the club and was inducted into the English Hall of Fame in 2007. He spent 14 years as the reserve team manager and had a short spell as caretaker in 2010. He also won 59 caps for his country, playing at two World Cups and a Euros.

Across

1. He finished a match as the stand-in goalkeeper for Newcastle against this club. (4,3,6)

3. Beardsley served as assistant manager for England to him. (6,9)

5. Beardsley made a single appearance for this Premier League club in 1982. (10,6)

14. Canadian side that he had three spells at during his career. (9,9)

18. The arrival of this Israel striker limited Beardsley's first team opportunities at Liverpool. (5,9)

19. Strike partner who he scored a combined 65 goals with in all competitions in the 1993/94 season. (4,4)

20. He finally ended his career at the age of 38 when he played twice for the Melbourne Knights in this country.

Down

2. County Durham club who were his last in England. (10,6)

4. He began his league career at this Cumbrian side. (8,6)

6. His first goals at St James' Park were against this team, who he had a loan spell at in 1998. (10,4)

7. He left Newcastle a second time in 1997 to join this club. (6,9)

8. He dropped back into the Newcastle midfield after they signed this striker. (4,7)

9. He took over as caretaker manager of Newcastle after the sacking of this man. (5,7)

10. Manager and former teammate who re-signed him for Newcastle. (5,6)

11. Club he won two First Division titles and an FA Cup with.

12. His first goal for Newcastle was against this Welsh club. (7,4)

13. Along with this player they are the only two players to have scored for both sides in Merseyside derbies. (5,7)

15. England strike partner who described him as "the best partner I could ever have". (4,7)

16. Manchester United striker who appeared in the 1993/94 Premier League Team of the Season up front alongside Beardsley. (4,7)

17. Beardsley's final competitive goal for Liverpool was against this club who he was then controversially sold to.

Round 17 - Steve Harper & Shay Given

Steve Harper spent an incredible 20 years with the club and was competing with Shay Given for 12 of those. Combined they racked up 661 games including some Champions League appearances. How much do you know about these two loyal stoppers?

Across

1. Newcastle honoured Harper for his 20 years at the club with a testimonial against this Italian side. (2.5)

3. Given joined this club after leaving Newcastle. (10.4)

5. Given began his career at this club.

6. Given was signed by Newcastle from this club. (9.6)

10. Club that Given and Harper both played for other than Newcastle.

11. Harper joined this Championship side on a one-month loan in October 2011. (8.3.4.6)

15. Given's real first name.

16. Harper broke Newcastle's clean sheet record for a season with his nineteenth clean sheet in March 2010 against this Yorkshire club. (9.6)

17. Given is the second-highest capped Republic of Ireland player with 134 caps, behind only this player. (6.5)

18. Given got his 100th cap for Ireland against this Balkan nation.

19. Liverpool goalkeeper who was Harper's idol. (5.10)

Down

1. Harper played his last game for Newcastle against this London club.

2. Given suffered a one-centimetre tear in his bowel after a tackle by this West Ham striker in 2006. (6.8)

4. Given's 400th appearance for Newcastle was against this club in January 2007. (10.6)

7. Given overtook this player as having played the most European matches for Newcastle in September 2004. (4.7)

8. Liverpool player who scored from inside his own half against Harper in 2006. (4.6)

9. Harper said the highlight of his career was winning the Championship title which was confirmed with a win at this Devon club. (8.6)

12. Given's Premier League debut and Harper's Newcastle debut both came against this London club.

13. Harper made his 50th consecutive league start for Newcastle in 2010 against this Yorkshire club (his longest run of consecutive starts he had made in his career).

14. Given made his 400th league appearance against this club in October 2009 who he later spent four seasons at. (5.5)

Round 18 - General I

You've done well to reach this point: I hope you have learnt lots of cool facts about Newcastle United. Here are three rounds of general questions from a range of categories to finish off. Good luck!

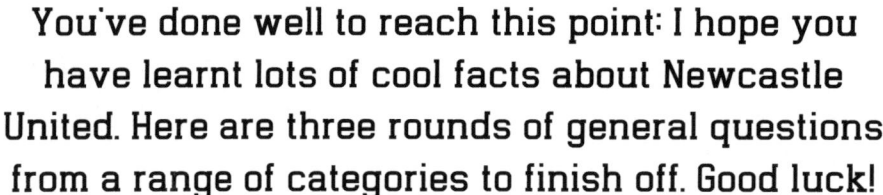

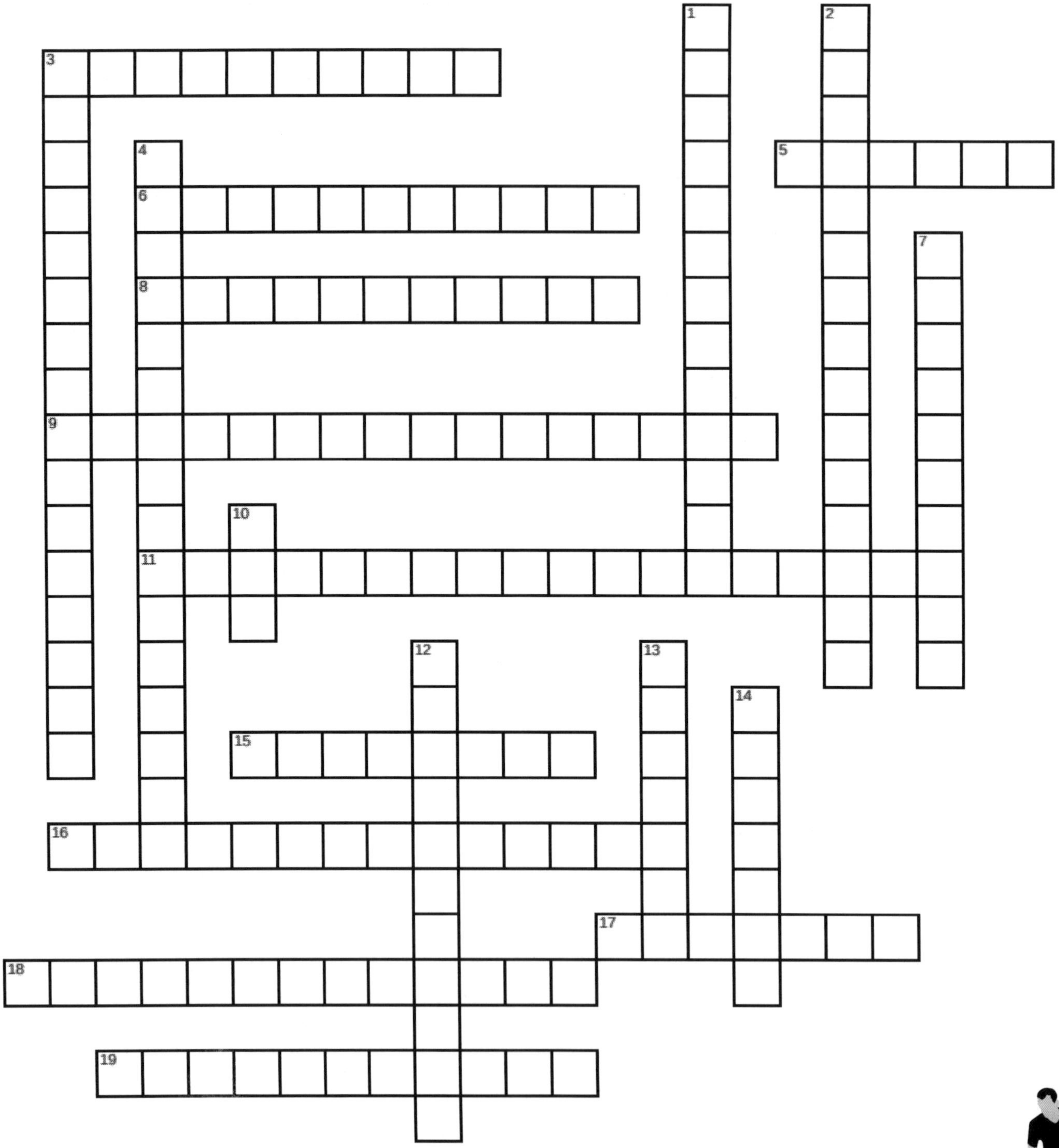

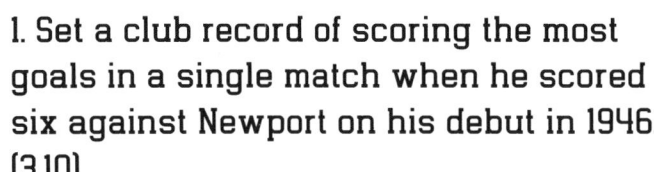

Across

3. Newcastle's nickname. (3.7)

5. Joelinton's country of birth.

6. The bar beneath the upper tier of the Gallowgate End is named after this legend. (4.7)

8. Newcastle's last game before the Covid-19 crowd restrictions was a 1-0 away win against this team.

9. Newcastle finished runners-up to this club in the 1995/96 league season. (10.6)

11. Steve Bruce managed this club before joining Newcastle. (9.9)

15. He was the first player to wear Newcastle's number nine shirt in the Premier League era. (4.4)

16. The club's top scorer in the 2006/07 season.

17. Welsh Hall of Famer who played for Newcastle in the 1997/98 season. (3.4)

18. Newcastle played their first match under their new title of Newcastle United against this local rival after the merger.

19. The only African player to have made over 200 Premier League appearances for Newcastle. (5.6)

Down

1. Set a club record of scoring the most goals in a single match when he scored six against Newport on his debut in 1946. (3.10)

2. Temuri Ketsbaia was given this nickname by the Newcastle fans. (8.7)

3. The first game after the Saudi takeover was a 3-2 home loss to this side. (9.7)

4. Famously scored a hat-trick as Newcastle beat Barcelona 3-2 in the Champions League. (8.8)

7. The only English player signed by Ruud Gullit during his spell as manager. (6.4)

10. Newcastle's original colours were white and ___. (3)

12. This player scored 8 goals for England while playing for Newcastle. (7.4)

13. The record home attendance of 68,386 was against this London club in September 1930.

14. Newcastle's first ever penalty shoot-out victory came against this club in a League Cup game in 2006.

Round 19 - General II

Across

2. The club's 10th highest scorer of all-time with 97 goals between 1962-71. (3.6)

4. Apart from Newcastle this is the only other team to qualify for the Champions League 2nd round after losing their first three games. doing so in 2019.

10. Scored the first Newcastle goal of the Saudi-era. (6.6)

16. Newcastle bought David Ginola in 1995 from this club. (5.5.7)

17. Has the most Premier League assists for Newcastle. (8.6)

18. This player scored the winning goal as Newcastle lost 4-3 to Liverpool in April 1996 to suffer a major blow in the title race. (4.9)

19. Club that Papiss Cisse was signed from.

20. Newcastle's record transfer before the world record transfer of Alan Shearer in 1996. (3.9)

Down

1. Irishman signed from Chelsea in 2006 for £5m. (6.4)

3. Callum Wilson and Matt Ritchie came in from this club.

5. Newcastle were ahead of Man United by this many points in mid-January 1996 before going on to finish second at the end of the season.

6. This player joined Newcastle from Man United as part of the deal that took Andy Cole the other way. (5.9)

7. Won the 2015 Player of the Year. (5.7)

8. Newcastle hold the joint record for most draws in the Premier League season with 17 draws alongside Sunderland and this other club. (5.5)

9. Japanese international signed from Mainz in 2018. (9.4)

11. Striker whose only league goal for the club came in a 4-1 victory at the Stadium of Light in 2006. (6.5)

12. Newcastle's record signing from 2005-2019. (7.4)

13. This player opened the scoring when Newcastle famously demolished Man United 5-0 in 1996. (6.7)

14. Premier League referee from 2004-17 who was unable to referee Newcastle games as he is a big fan of the club. (4.11)

15. Chris Waddle scored a 24-minute hat-trick against this side as Newcastle raced to a 4-0 half time lead although the game finished 5-5 in September 1984. (6.4.7)

Round 20 - General III

Across

1. Ivorian who rose to fame due to the FIFA video games series who had a loan spell from CSKA Moscow in 2016. (6.7)

5. Czech goalkeeper is the oldest player to represent Newcastle in the Premier League. (5.7)

8. Slovenian forward who made just 19 league appearances during his seven-year spell before leaving in 2017. (5.6)

9. Frenchman who had a twelve-game spell with the club before more successful spells at Fulham, Man United and Everton. (5.4)

11. Midfielder signed from Swansea City in 2016. (5.7)

13. Newcastle have been drawn the most times in cup games against this Midlands team. (10.6)

14. Became the first player from Cyprus to play for Newcastle in 1993. (9.12)

15. This West Ham defender scored a hat-trick against Newcastle in 1986 against three different keepers. (5.6)

16. US-born Italian striker who had a thirteen-game loan spell from Man United in 2006. (8.5)

17. National team of Christian Atsu.

18. Striker nicknamed the 'Flying Finn', signed as a replacement for Andy Carroll. (6.4)

Down

1. This Newcastle United photographer had the idea of inventing the windscreen wiper while driving back from the club's FA Cup Final against Wolves in 1907. (9.5)

4. This player was signed from Milan in 1998 before leaving to join AIK a year later. (7.9)

6. Known as the "Clown Prince of Soccer", he is generally regarded as one of English football's finest ever entertainers having made his name at Sunderland after joining from Newcastle. (3.10)

7. Since the retirement of Alan Shearer he has scored the most Premier League goals for Newcastle. (6.5)

10. Defender signed from Leeds in 2003 and sold to Real Madrid a year later. (8.8)

12. He has the highest goals/games percentage strike rate for Newcastle at 82%. (6.9)

Answers

Round 1 - Founding & History

Round 2 - 1950/60s

Round 3 - 1970/80s

Across

1 TOTTENHAMHOTSPUR
4 LIVERPOOL
7 PAULGASCOIGNE
8 SOUTHAMPTON
14 QUEENSPARKRANGERS
17 OSSIEARDILES
18 CHRISWADDLE
19 BURNLEY

Down

2 MALCOLMMACDONALD
3 MIRANDINHA
5 JACKCHARLTON
6 PETERWITHE
8 SAMALLARDYCE
9 PETERBEARDSLEY
10 MICKMARTIN
11 LIVERPOOL
12 ALANGOWLING
13 IMREVARADI
15 STJOHNSTON
16 JIMMYSMITH

Round 4 – 1990s

Round 5 - 2000s

Round 6 - 2010s

Crossword answers:
- 3 Across: JAMESPERCH
- 4 Across: JOELINTON
- 6 Across: JOEYBARTON
- 8 Across: SALOMONRONDON
- 9 Across: ADAMCAMPBELL
- 11 Across: FABRICIOCOLOCCINI
- 12 Across: KEVINNOLAN
- 14 Across: SOLCAMPBELL
- 15 Across: NORWICHCITY
- 17 Across: AYOZEPEREZ
- 18 Across: LOICREMY
- 19 Across: TIMKRUL

- 1 Down: CHEIKTIOTE
- 2 Down: LEONBEST
- 5 Down: WESTHAMUNITED
- 6 Down: JAALLASCELLES
- 7 Down: PAPISSCISSE
- 10 Down: DWIGHTGAYLE
- 13 Down: ANDYCARROL
- 16 Down: FRANCE

Round 7 - 2020s

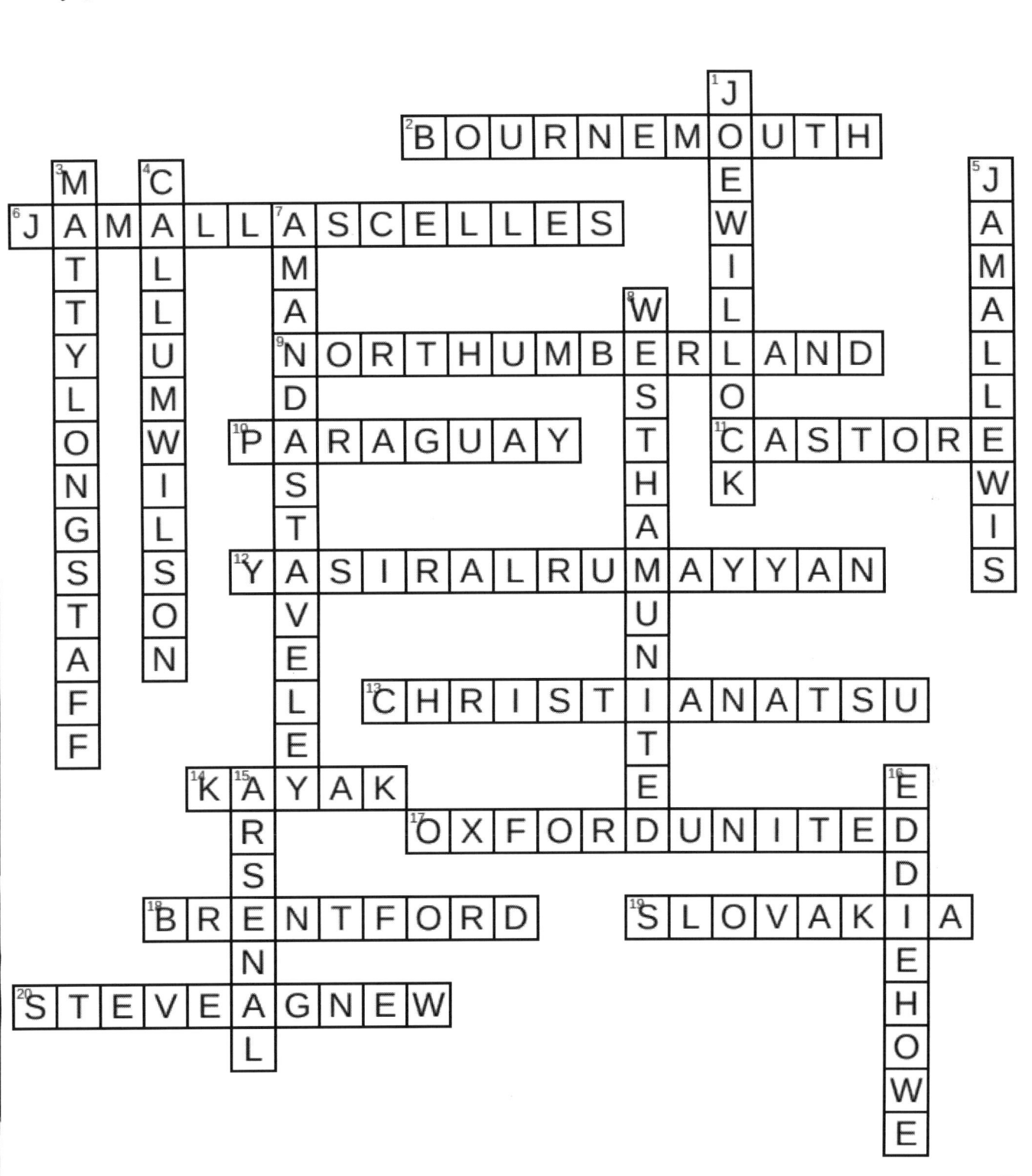

Round 8 - Stan Seymour & Joe Harvey

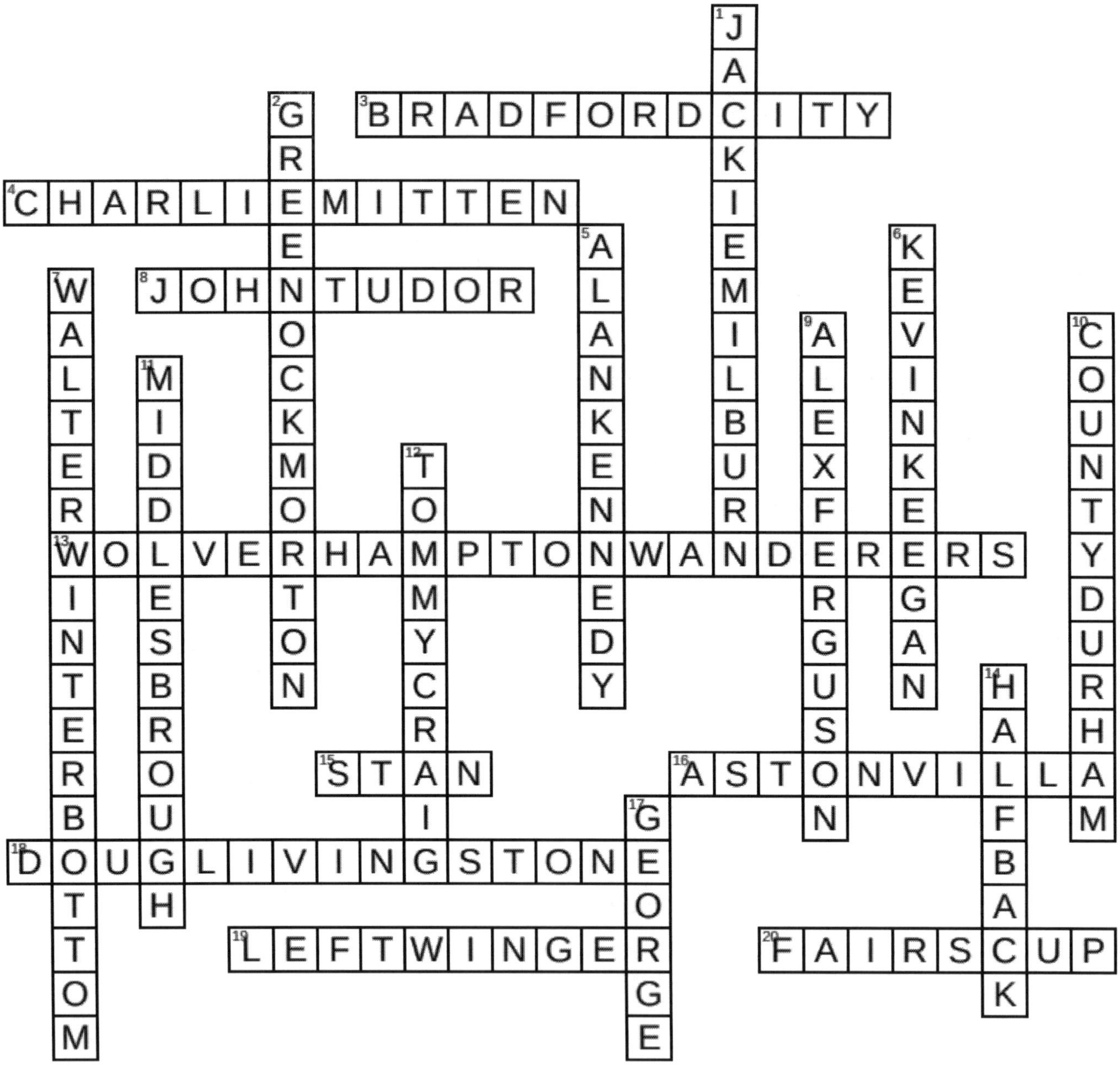

Round 9 - Managers

Across:
2. RAFA BENITEZ
3. JOE HARVEY
5. JOE KINNEAR
6. JOHN CARVER
7. ALAN PARDEW
9. KENNY DALGLISH
14. BOBBY ROBSON
20. DOUG LIVINGSTONE

Down:
1. JACK CHARLTON
4. RICHARD DINNIS
8. ALAN SHEARER
10. GRAEME SOUNESS
11. CHRIS HUGHTON
12. SAM ALLARDYCE
13. GLENN ROEDER
15. BOBBY SAIRDILES
16. GORDON LEE
17. STEVE CLARKE
18. RUUD GULLIT
19. TOMMY MATHER

Round 10 - Jackie Milburn

Round 11 - Alan Shearer

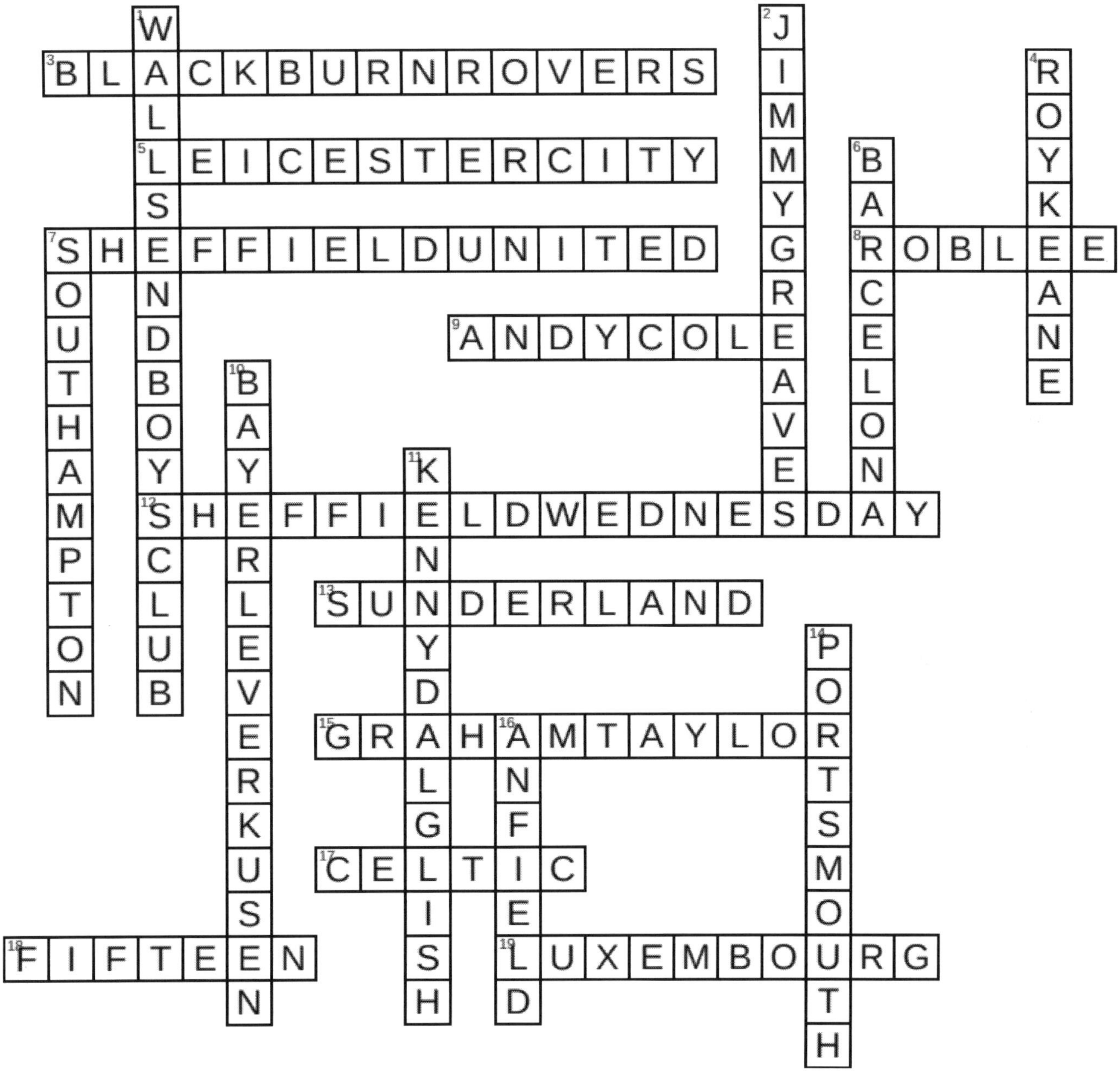

Across
- 3. BLACKBURN ROVERS
- 5. LEICESTER CITY
- 7. SHEFFIELD UNITED
- 8. ROB LEE
- 9. ANDY COLE
- 12. SHEFFIELD WEDNESDAY
- 13. SUNDERLAND
- 15. GRAHAM TAYLOR
- 17. CELTIC
- 18. FIFTEEN
- 19. LUXEMBOURG

Down
- 1. WALSALL SANDBOY CLUB
- 2. JIMMY GREAVES
- 4. ROY KEANE
- 6. BARCELONA
- 7. SOUTHAMPTON
- 10. BAYER LEVERKUSEN
- 11. KENNY DALGLISH
- 14. PORTSMOUTH
- 16. ANFIELD

Round 12 – St James' Park

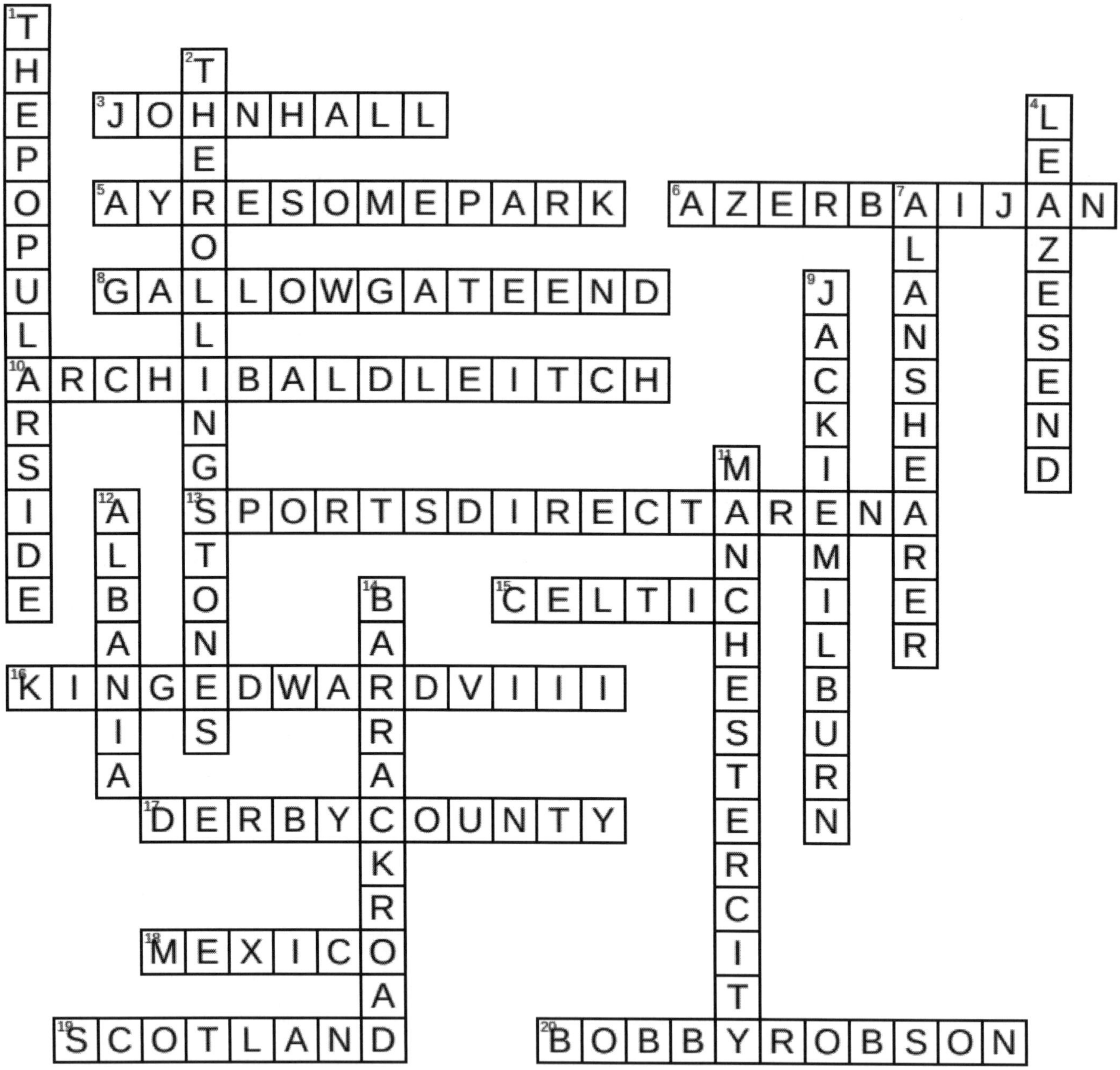

Round 13 - Academy Graduates

Across:
2. Fraser Forster
4. Adam Armstrong
5. Steven Taylor
6. Steve Watson
8. Robbie Elliott
9. James Tavernier
11. Aaron Hughes
12. Andy Carroll
14. Steven Caldwell
15. Michael Chopra
16. Tim Krul
17. Sean Longstaff
18. Nile Ranger

Down:
1. Freddie
3. Paul Gascoigne
4. Adidi (Shola Ameobi)
5. Shola Ameobi
7. Steve Howey
8. Rob Wood (Robbie Wood...)
10. Paul Dummett
12. Alan Thompson
13. Lee Clark

Round 14 - Club Captains

Round 15 - Kevin Keegan

Round 16 - Peter Beardsley

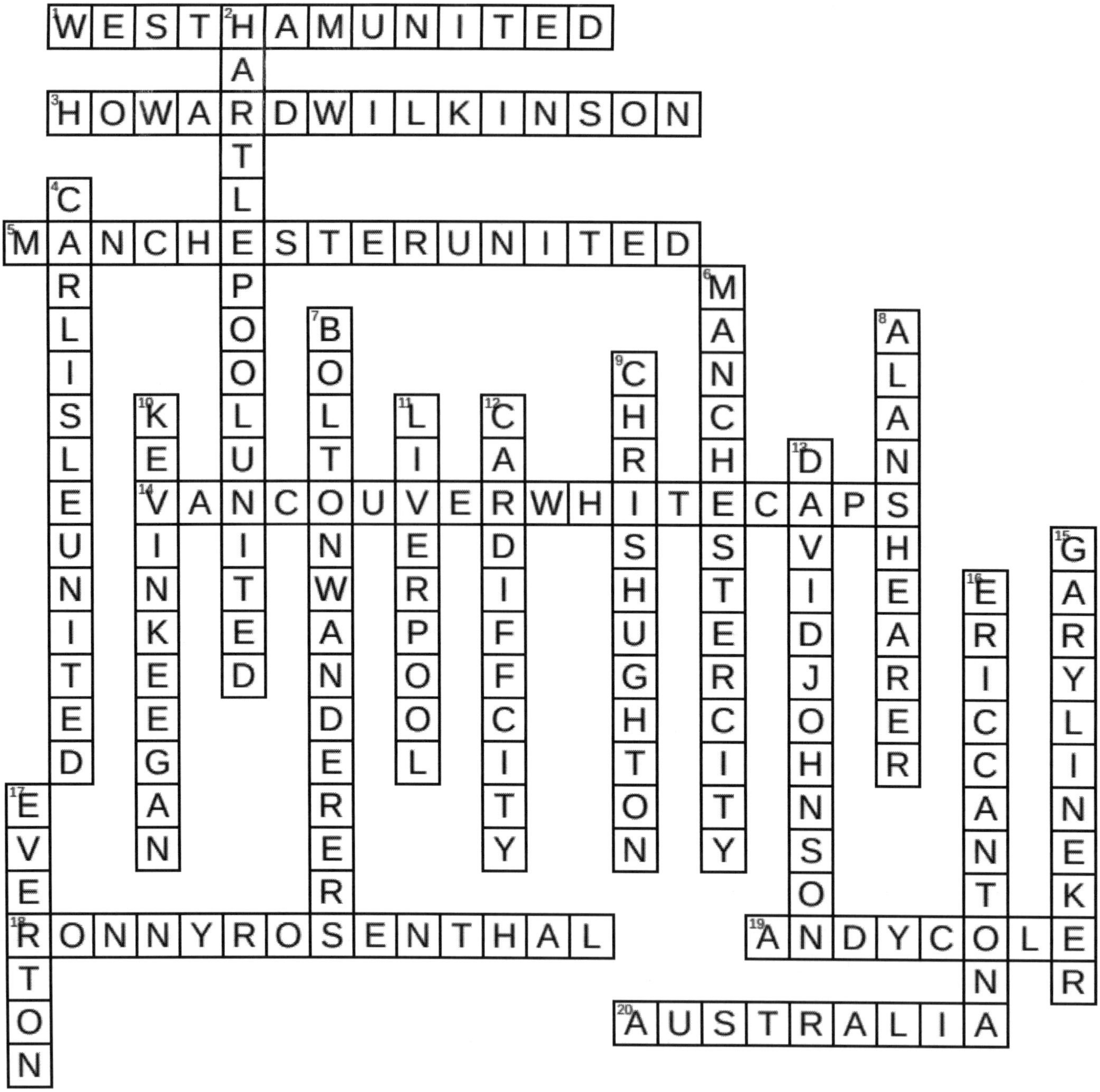
1 WESTHAMUNITED
2 HARTLEPOOLUNITED
3 HOWARDWILKINSON
4 CARLISLEUNITED
5 MANCHESTERUNITED
6 MANCHESTERCITY
7 BOLTONWANDERERS
8 ALANSHEARER
9 CHRISHUGHTON
10 KEVINKEEGAN
11 LIVERPOOL
12 CARDIFFCITY
13 DAVIDJOHNSON
14 VANCOUVERWHITECAPS
15 GARYLINEKER
16 ERICCANTONA
17 EVERTON
18 RONNYROSENTHAL
19 ANDYCOLE
20 AUSTRALIA

Round 17 - Shay Given & Steve Harper

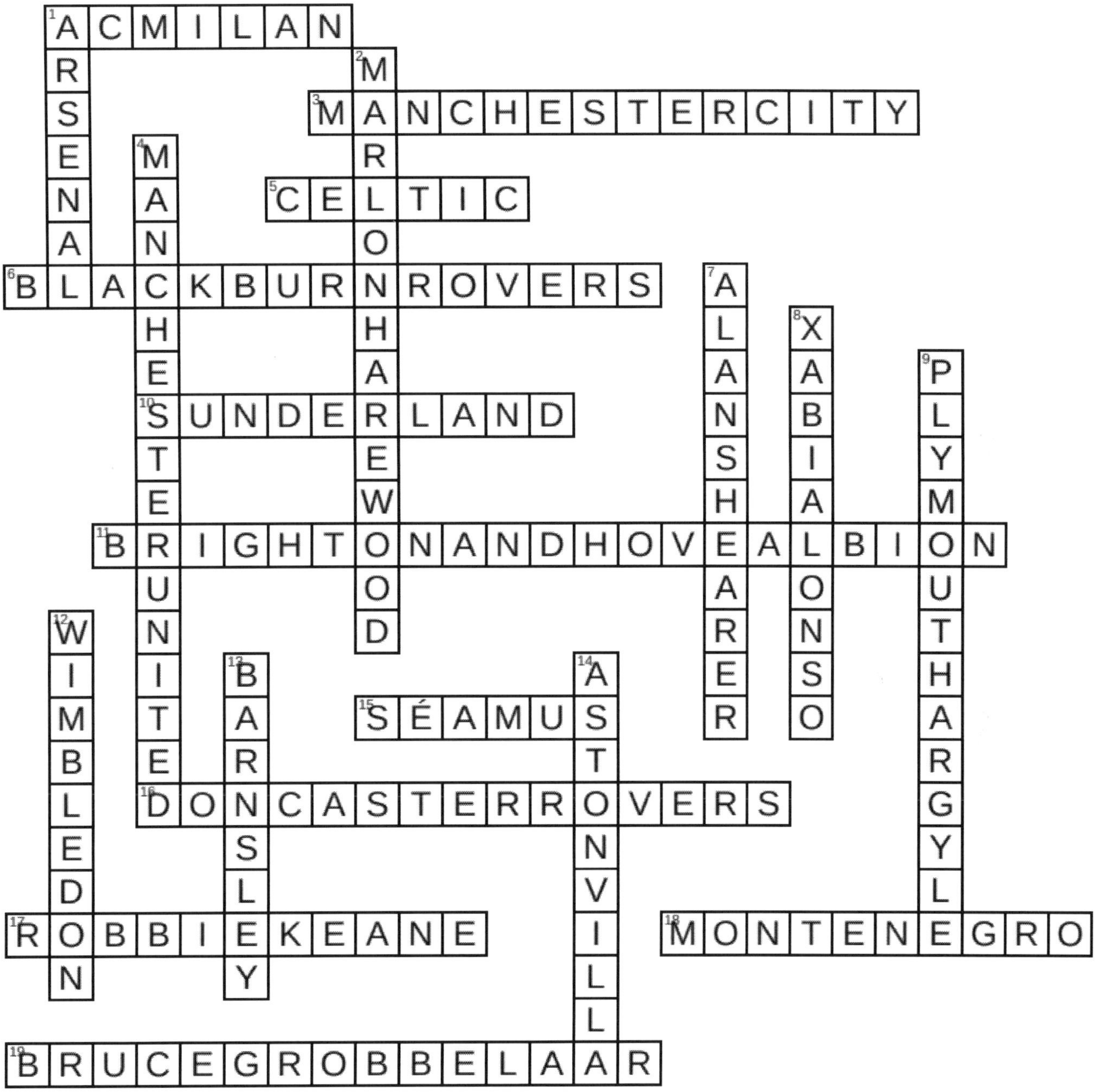

Round 18 - General I

Across
- 3. THE MAGPIES
- 5. BRAZIL
- 6. ALAN SHEARER
- 8. SOUTHAMPTON
- 9. MANCHESTER UNITED
- 11. SHEFFIELD WEDNESDAY
- 15. ANDY COLE
- 16. OBAFEMI MARTINS
- 17. IAN RUSH
- 18. MIDDLESBROUGH
- 19. SHOLA AMEOBI

Down
- 1. LEN SHACKLETON
- 2. GEORGI␣ANGEORDIE
- 3. TOTTENHAM HOTSPUR
- 4. FAUSTINO␣ASPRILLA
- 7. KIERON␣DYER
- 10. RED
- 12. MICHAEL␣OWEN
- 13. CHELSEA
- 14. WATFORD

Round 19 - General II

Round 20 - General III

That's all folks, thank you so much for purchasing this Newcastle crossword book. I really hope you enjoyed it and learnt some cool facts about the club to impress your fellow Magpies.

As a small independent publisher any reviews you can leave will be a big help as I try to grow my company and produce better and better books for you to enjoy.

If you have any criticisms, please do email me before leaving a negative review and I'd be happy to assist you if you have any problems!

kieran.brown2402@gmail.com

Printed in Great Britain
by Amazon